DESIGN
and decorate
KITCHENS

Lesley Taylor

Adams Media Corporation
Holbrook, Massachusetts

This edition published by Adams Media Corporation
260 Center Street
Holbrook, MA 02343
by arrangement with New Holland (Publishers) Ltd.

ISBN-1-55850-838-4

Taylor, Lesley
Design and decorate kitchens / Lesley Taylor.
p. cm.
Includes index.
ISBN 1-55850-838-4 (alk. paper)
1. Kitchens–Planning. 2. Kitchens– Design and construction.
3. Kitchens–Equipment and supplies. 4. Interior decoration.
I. Title.
TX653. T38 1998   97-41185
647.95–dc21   CIP

Printed and bound in Singapore

Contents

Introduction

I have been involved with many kitchen designs during my career, but it seems rather appropriate that while I was writing this book I was re-planning and extending the kitchen in my own home. Although many of you may think that it must be very easy for interior designers to design for their own house, I can assure you, when you have too much information it can be more difficult to make the decisions needed. Planning my kitchen, then, has given me an insight into how it feels when asked to make the choices that will affect your home. I hope this is reflected in the way the book has been written, giving you information in a very practical and helpful manner, with a few personal experiences added for good measure.

Design and Decorate Kitchens has been written to give you an insight into the world of kitchen design, explaining the styles now available and showing how they can be adapted to best suit your family and home. Conceptualizing – the planning and layout of your kitchen – is examined, giving you the knowledge and confidence to design your own kitchen or to understand and converse intelligently with any kitchen designer you choose to work with. The Focus File section on pages 60-77 then looks at the elements needed to complete a kitchen. Wallcoverings, flooring, worktops and lighting are all looked at in detail, ensuring you have all the information to make educated decisions that will avoid costly mistakes. My advice is to take your time and enjoy creating this all-important part of your home.

Layout *and* planning

GOOD DESIGN
▲ The positioning of the main appliances in the kitchen is very important. The stove, refrigerator and sink should all be readily accessible and within an acceptable distance of each other.

ROOM TO WORK
► This chic modern kitchen offers ample work surfaces around the main food preparation area, something that is very important in a well-planned kitchen.

Good layout and planning are the keys to a successful kitchen. Decorative styles and aesthetic considerations are, of course, important. But the time spent on planning the room can make the difference between a nicely decorated kitchen and one that is not only decoratively pleasing but also functional, comfortable and "user-friendly".

The best layout for your kitchen very much depends on the individual needs of your particular family, so invest time in making a list of the facilities that your finished kitchen must offer to fulfill your requirements successfully. Some of the questions you may wish to consider are: Is your kitchen purely for the preparation and storage of food? Will you need to incorporate laundry facilities into the design? Do you need to include a dining area, and if so, is it purely for family eating or will you also use the space for entertaining guests? Will the space be used as a home study or for your children? Do you want the room to be multifunctional, with space for a television and seating area? Will it be the main room in the home and used throughout the day for food preparation, working and child minding?

Once you have established the main functions of your new kitchen, you can consider your personal preferences as to the finished look and atmosphere of the room, the style of appliances and the amount of storage you would like.

DIVIDED UP
◄ A beautifully crafted storage unit acts as a visual divide between the dining and cooking areas in this cottage-type kitchen.

Certain styles of kitchens lend themselves to particular situations. Modern kitchens have easy-to-clean surfaces and incorporate the best storage options, making them ideal for a growing family. The country or cottage kitchen, on the other hand, may not offer the same variety of storage, but it does create a very relaxed atmosphere – ideal for those who enjoy a more laid-back lifestyle. Whatever style of kitchen appeals to you, consider the options available within that genre, and spend time deciding which one will best fit the requirements that you have listed for your ideal kitchen.

Once your preferences are clear in your mind you must then decide if you feel confident enough to plan your own kitchen or whether you would rather leave the layout and planning to an

CAREFUL PLANNING

▲ Narrow galley kitchens need careful planning to maximize the space. Here is a tried and tested layout with ample work-surfaces and all the facilities close at hand.

expert in kitchen design. Kitchen designers will visit your home to discuss your requirements, gaining enough information to produce a plan and layout that they feel will best meet your individual needs from within their range of products. Don't be afraid to shop around, and if you find a style of kitchen from one company that particularly appeals to you, but prefer the layout suggested by another, feel free to discuss these alternatives with the designer.

If you wish to plan the kitchen yourself, first make a scale drawing on paper. You will be amazed how different your room will appear on a flat piece of paper, and how alternative layouts will become more apparent as you rearrange the elements on your plan.

Choose a convenient scale such as 1:20. This means that each inch on the plan represents 20 inches in your kitchen. Measure the room using a metal tape measure and draw the plan onto graph paper. Include any permanent fixtures, such as doors, radiators and windows. Then, using the same scale, draw out the proportions of your preferred storage units and appliances, cut these out and name or number them for ease of identification. You can then explore the layout options available to you.

Consideration must be given to the plumbing and electrical facilities within the room, but don't be restricted by what is already installed. The simple relocation of a sink unit, for example, can have a great effect on the finished layout. Traditionally, many kitchen designers placed the sink in front of a window, presumably to give the person doing the dishes an interesting outlook. But as many kitchens now have dishwashers, thankfully, considerably less time is spent on tasks by the sink. You may decide to use this area to position a dining table or breakfast bar, giving diners a brighter outlook.

Finally, don't be fooled by the idea that more is better: it only works if all the appliances are grouped together. In a well-designed kitchen, the quality of the layout outweighs the quantity of the units.

ULTRA CHIC
▲ Cooking appliances are the key components of any kitchen. In a modern environment you will want streamlined units with a minimum of fuss. This ultra-chic stainless steel griddle is based on a Japanese design and cooks food swiftly without additional fat.

WICKER WORK
▼ Wicker baskets are very fashionable and they provide an excellent storage option for fresh produce, allowing air to circulate.

STYLE *file*

In many houses the kitchen is considered the center of the home, a room in which the daily meals are prepared, the family gather to talk and eat, and a space where children can play and do their homework. So ample consideration must be given to planning and design, to ensure your kitchen can successfully fulfill the requirements of all the family.

A large percentage of accidents in the home occur in the kitchen, so when choosing fixtures, think about both their aesthetic qualities and their safety. Certain types of flooring, like highly polished marble, for example, can look simply stunning in a modern kitchen. But if such a floor gets wet it can be a very dangerous surface. If yours is a busy family kitchen, it will have to withstand more wear and tear than that of a retired couple, say, so surfaces should be both hard-wearing and easy to clean. Keep this uppermost in your mind when designing your kitchen, as some products are more appropriate than others, depending on your circumstances. The cottage style, for example, may contain rustic pine or oak furniture and terracotta, slate or stone flooring, and while these combine to create a very welcoming atmosphere – ideal for a family – they also require more maintenance than a contemporary look with its easily cleaned cabinets and hygienic ceramic or vinyl floors.

When selecting your kitchen, consider how the elements combine to create a look that will complement the style of your home and offer a practical and safe solution for your needs.

TOP LEFT
The old and the new make a winning combi nation. Traditional materials such as granite and wood team with stainless steel and modern paint effects.

BOTTOM LEFT
Freestanding cabinets and a mixture of painted furniture make this country house-style kitchen warm and inviting – a place to dine as well as to cook.

TOP RIGHT
This well-designed small kitchen uses laminated units and practical stainless steel. A wooden bar area fits snugly on one wall to create eating space.

BOTTOM RIGHT
The warmth of beech wood combined with cool chrome gives a relaxed, yet modern look. Spot-lighting draws the eye to a pair of uniquely patterned wall unit doors.

Traditional style

Traditional kitchens are those decorated with elements or themes derived from the past, but today many leading kitchen designers are mixing old themes with contemporary elements. The results are kitchens that work equally well in both traditional and modern homes. As with all good design, the best-decorated rooms need not be totally pure in style. In fact, a blend of complementary elements, such as materials made from wood and stone combined with paneling and carving, creates a very individual room.

If you wish to create a traditionally decorated room, then the items with the greatest influence on the finished look must be truly traditional. Individuality can then be achieved with the addition of smaller items in different styles.

CLEAR-CUT LINES

▶ This kitchen is simple yet practical, offering ample storage in an individual style. The cabinet doors have been made from tongue and groove boards and painted in neutral tones for a classic feel. Traditional door hardware in black iron give an authentic, old-fashioned touch.

PINE AND TERRACOTTA

▲ Antique pine lends a mellow warmth to any kitchen and this stylish room combines the beauty of natural wood and terracotta. Integrated modern appliances such as a refrigerator and dishwasher can be concealed within the run of cabinets, keeping the lines of the kitchen as simple and traditional as possible.

OLD AND NEW

◀ Traditional elements, such as the Belfast or butler's sink, are enjoying a revival, and combine well with a built-in range.

Clever color accents
in a traditional

I particularly love what are best called "personally styled" rooms. These are rooms that have been decorated to create a look that does not fall into a particular style or period but simply portrays the designer's or client's personality and individual taste.

Occasionally, a leading designer will create a particular look that then starts a trend. It is very difficult to analyze what makes this type of room successful, as by its very nature it does not fall into any one category. Sometimes there is no specific reason for individual elements combining to create a pleasing room — they just do.

The room featured here is just such an example. Traditional rustic pine has been combined with Victorian-style painted furniture to create a unique kitchen. The strongest elements in the kitchen are the crimson-painted base and wall cabinets in the center of the far wall; the additional storage units look almost incidental by their side. The mock dresser, made especially striking by using a brilliant brick red paint, is the focal point of the room, as it would be in a more conventional kitchen. The continuous wooden worktops also link the various colored base units effectively to create a sense of unity.

The result is a totally functional, built-in kitchen,

THE BEAUTY OF WOOD
◀ Mix painted and natural wood to create the look achieved here. Combine old and new woods, waxing, staining or varnishing them as you wish and teaming them with freshly painted surfaces. Use an eggshell, gloss or satin oil-based paint for a durable finish.

wooden kitchen

but because of the variations in colors and textures, it has an eclectic, old-fashioned atmosphere. It is a good example of a kitchen that combines the old and the new in an understated way.

This type of kitchen would work especially well in a country cottage where the occupier feels comfortable with all styles of traditional furniture. It would look equally good in a townhouse if the occupant has a love for country simplicity and is looking for a style that blends in with the architecture of a period home.

COLOR THEORY
▲ Consider the effect that color can have on the balance of the finished room.
A knowledge of color theory can be very helpful here, as the use of certain colors could make a room appear longer or wider. In general, warm colors advance and cool colors recede.

Soft shades revive
an old kitchen

A few years ago, kitchen designers looked for inspiration to the traditional cook's kitchen found in the servants' quarters of large, old houses. This led to a revival of the painted wooden kitchen. The old kitchens were very well designed, with ample storage and whole walls of cabinets and drawers. The up-to-date version of this area offers the home a well-organized space with a traditional air. The cream color associated with this style of kitchen is still very popular, but has also given way to a more contemporary range of colors, giving the basic design a modern feel.

The kitchen featured here is the perfect example of a new style of cook's kitchen where striking color combinations are mixed with traditional pieces of furniture to create a warm and welcoming family space. The beauty of this sort of kitchen is its ability to work well in so many different types of house. It looks equally at home in a small, surburban house as it does in a large country manor.

Appliances such as dishwashers are housed in matching cabinets to help retain the character of this kind of kitchen. While most styles of cooktop and oven would work successfully in this setting, traditional ranges, like the one featured opposite, fully enhance the design features that were originally part of this type of kitchen.

This particular color scheme uses light yellow

INDIVIDUAL CERAMICS
▶ Ceramic tiles have a rich and interesting history. Originating in Persia and China, it was many hundreds of years before glazed tiles were used in Europe. Today, many manufacturers and some individual potteries offer handmade tiles made by traditional methods.

painted walls as a summery backdrop behind the peppermint green cabinets and painted furniture. Schemes featuring traditional wallpapers or stenciling would be equally successful. If you choose this option, use vinyl-coated wallpapers to withstand the moisture created by cooking. Likewise, use paints that are specifically designed for steamy kitchen use. The tiled walls behind the work surfaces and cooking area are a practical – as well as decorative – finishing touch, as they are quick to put up and easy to wipe down.

CHANGING THE COLORS

▲ Painted kitchens always offer the option of restyling, as you can simply change the color in years to come. This means you can give your room a new lease of life without installing a new kitchen. Simply sand the original woodwork lightly to enable the new paint to adhere, and apply at least two coats of a suitable paint.

Old-fashioned charm from *traditional materials*

This beautiful, sunlit kitchen includes all the elements associated with traditional styling: stone, wicker, mellow golden wood and painted walls. Yet because of the style of the wooden kitchen cabinets it has a refreshingly modern feel. While other elements of this room are very rustic in character, these clean-lined cabinets look completely at home because they are made from natural wood. Natural wood acts very well as a bridge between two distinctive styles. The same basic shape manufactured in a different material would look completely out of place in this setting.

The room has a wonderful feeling of spaciousness, due to plentiful natural light. This is also enhanced by the lack of wall cabinets. Instead, an open-style plate rack offers additional storage without completely dominating the wall area.

This kitchen offers the best of both worlds, the relaxed atmosphere associated with a traditional setting but the practical advantages that come from modern styling. Items like the cast-iron sink and the granite work surfaces have been chosen not only because of their association with the traditional kitchen but because they are so practical. Likewise, the wicker baskets form ideal storage containers for fresh produce as they allow air to circulate freely.

The basic color scheme of this room falls into the natural or neutral category. This group of colors ranges from browns and creams through to whites, and appear on a regular basis with

NATURAL SURFACES

▲ In place of a granite worktop consider marble or ceramic tiles, each of which is hard-wearing, easy to clean and available in a great range of colors and styles.

and greenery

each new trend, mainly because they are so easy to live with. While this type of color scheme is often full of texture and warmth, it can look bland unless there is plenty of tonal variety in the room. This means adjusting the depths of color to add interest and dimension to the basic scheme. Imagine this room as a black and white picture and you will see what is meant by tonal variety. Even the stenciled border offers a change in tone. Another tip to pep up a neutral scheme is to add an "accent" color. Here, the plants offer the perfect solution, providing a much-needed splash of green to the room.

SUNLIT KITCHEN

◀ In this warm and sunny kitchen, stone tiling provides a cool and practical floor covering. Although an expensive option, stone floors are extremely durable and can be softened with a rug or natural matting.

Sage and ivory
team in a practical

CONCEALED STORAGE

▲ A refrigerator is cleverly concealed behind panels that match the cabinets.

QUICK CHANGE

▼ One of the simplest ways to change the style of a kitchen is to replace the cabinet hardware. Try specialist door furniture suppliers for a really wide range.

The kitchen is undoubtedly one of the most expensive rooms in the home to decorate, and that is why many people look for one that will not go out of fashion very quickly. This is another reason for the popularity of traditional kitchens, as these are classics that have successfully passed the test of time.

The kitchen featured here relies on excellent craftsmanship and good traditional design to give the room its distinctive, ageless quality. This does not mean, however, that the cabinets are historical reproductions. In fact, there are a number of design details incorporated by the designer to make this cook's kitchen very much a room for today. Not only are the best working appliances and cooking facilities supplied, but there are certain elements that have been exaggerated in proportion to add an interesting twist to the overall look of the finished room. The substantial curved cornices, for example, are a refreshing change from the normal mitered corner detail that is normally associated with this style of fitting. The drawer knobs, too, are larger than you would expect to find on surfaces of this size. The overall effect of these details is stylish, practical and full of individuality.

Color also plays a big part in the design of this kitchen. Sage green has been chosen as the primary color, with cream to add relief and natural tones for contrast. The base cabinets provide the main block of color with a dash of cream added via the door knobs. The Corian counter is also

cook's kitchen

cream, keeping the overall look very crisp and fresh. Above this begins a backsplash of Delft-influenced ceramic tiles that reach to the ceiling, again in sage and cream. These create a soft background pattern while providing a practical and easy-to-clean wall covering. Note how a molding tile has been positioned at picture rail height to add a traditional detail to the room.

The cream wall cabinets are mounted in front of this patterned backdrop. The designer has chosen this pale color to keep the look as airy as possible. This is most important where the run of cabinets is confined mainly to one wall. If the wall cabinets were sage, the balance of the room would be lost.

DARK AND LIGHT
▲ Sage and cream are combined in perfect balance to create a traditional kitchen with a modern slant.

Contemporary style

STREAMLINED
▲ Bright blocks of color and straight runs of cabinets make this kitchen truly contemporary.

Every few years there is a trend in interior design which, as with fashion, filters through from the leading designers and becomes mainstream taste. Over the last two decades we have seen a Victorian revival and the return of the country interior. But this has now made way for a new and refreshing trend that incorporates the bright and confident use of color and clean, simple lines. It is the return of the streamlined and hi-tech contemporary interior.

The word "contemporary" is described in the dictionary as being of the same age or era, which simply means this style is current or of this period. So by its very nature, contemporary design includes a number of up-to-date styles, including the clean, modern look that is now so popular. Choosing to decorate your kitchen in a contemporary way gives you a wide design spectrum to work within, along with the opportunity of being creative and individual.

If you are planning a contemporary kitchen, you may wish to choose brightly colored, highly glossed kitchen cabinets, or modular wooden furniture teamed with chrome and modern plastics. Whatever you choose, this style enables you to use bold color with confidence.

CHERRY WOOD AND BLACK PAINT
▶ One contemporary kitchen designer celebrates the style of the innovative and highly original Scottish designer and architect, Charles Rennie Mackintosh, with his interpretation of a "Mackintosh" kitchen.

INDUSTRIAL STYLE

▲ Many contemporary schemes include industrial-looking elements. This one includes chrome, glass and strong ocher-colored walls. Notice, too, the smooth-flowing, wavy lines of the vivid blue laminated kitchen cabinets.

CHROME AND GLASS

◄ Free-standing modular cabinets are readily available from a number of home improvement stores. They offer unlimited storage options in the modern home, particularly in a kitchen where attractive, practical shelf space is at a premium.

Natural textures and
neutral tones create

This stunning kitchen gives natural products like wood and slate a slick, modern look. The designer has harnessed all the beauty of natural wood, making its color variation and graining an important part of the kitchen design. This results in a mellow room with the wood's natural character adding design detail, as opposed to fussy paneling and moldings, for interest.

The mixing of textures within a room can add as much interest as the cleverest blending of patterns. Here, gray-green slate offers the room a very practical floor covering that

GRID LINES
▼ The elements of this kitchen make great use of squares and rectangles in the storage, flooring and the glass partition. The overall effect is one of simplicity and modernity.

chic, modern style

contrasts beautifully with the mellow, smooth texture of the wooden furniture. It also sits very comfortably alongside the simple white walls and glass block partition. All of these products have been chosen to add variation of texture, and therefore visual enhancement, to the room. The color palette is limited to neutral tones with shades of muted green on the marble work surfaces, stool cushions and slate floor.

Note how the far wall is fully appointed with elegant and streamlined cabinets from floor to ceiling. They keep the lines of the kitchen as simple as possible and also raise the ceiling height in the room. Indeed, simplicity is the key to this room's success and each element relies on its natural beauty to add detail to the room. There are no curtains, and no additional patterns to detract from the character brought by each individual carefully chosen item.

This is a kitchen designed for entertaining in style – there is ample storage for drinks, the glasses are within easy reach and the work tops have been specially designed to incorporate a wooden chopping block into the practical and easy-to-clean slate slabs. Chrome appliances and accessories are not just practical and smart — they help to enhance the modern feel of the kitchen. Each of these small details ensures that both entertaining and food preparation are as enjoyable as possible.

MODERN-DAY DISPLAY

◀ The concept of the traditional dresser to display kitchenware is still popular. Today, glass-fronted cupboards serve the same purpose and help to break up a run of wall cabinets.

STREAMLINED HEATING

▼ Keep the lines simple. Contemporary heating comes in the form of wall-mounted radiator panels, available in a wide range of colors.

Refreshing pastels
transform a small area

Most of us are now aware of the benefits of a kitchen/dining area – a room in which to relax and entertain as well as to prepare and eat meals. Some people relocate their kitchen to a larger room in the home, such as a rarely used formal dining room. If this is not the answer for you, then a single-story extension on an existing room, or a conservatory housing a working kitchen, may be the perfect solution. The pastel-painted kitchen featured here is an excellent example of a well-designed and compact kitchen positioned in a single-story extension to the side of a living space.

COLOR CONFIDENCE

▼ It is the confident use of color that lifts this kitchen from the mundane to the fabulous. The choice and balance of colors – pale mauve teamed with the palest creamy lemon and cobalt blue – can be carried from the overall decor through to the smaller details.

When planning a kitchen extension or refurbishment, it is a good idea to decide how much of your time will be spent preparing meals in the room, and how much time will be taken with activities more associated with a living or sitting room. If your kitchen is well designed, a great deal can be achieved in a very limited space: good planning is the key to a successful working kitchen (see pages 6-9). As much can be achieved by an organized cook in a small kitchen as in the most generous of spaces. You may therefore be surprised at how little space you need to allocate to the working kitchen. Really, all that is needed is adequate storage, a stove, refrigerator, sink and sufficient preparation and serving spaces.

The attractive kitchen featured here benefits from the additional natural light supplied by the skylights and further enhanced by the chosen color scheme. Lemon-green wall and base cabinets sit very happily on a lavender blue background. It is interesting to note that pastels are the only colors on the color wheel that you can guarantee will never clash; it doesn't matter what combination you team together, they will always work successfully. The lavender blue walls and ceiling also act to maximize the available space as all blue-based, cool colors appear to recede, and therefore create the impression of pushing back the walls that they decorate. Tonal interest is provided by the dark blue stained glass in the windows and the inset border on the tiled backsplash. This important detail acts to emphasize the area, adding depth to a basically pastel color scheme.

LAVENDER ISLAND

▲ The island unit provides an additional work surface and lots of storage; it also acts as a natural divide, between the working area of the kitchen and the dining or sitting room.

White and chrome
mellowed with

As with all color schemes, the lighter the colors used, the larger the area in which they appear will look. Here, a fairly narrow kitchen leading to a dining area has benefited from the use of pure white cabinets. Look at the area where the kitchen meets the dining room and imagine how tall and narrow the opening would have seemed if the units on either side had been a deeper color.

White can have the disadvantage of giving a room a clinical and sometimes cold appearance, especially in north-facing rooms. This is because blocks of white can appear gray when natural light lacks the sun's warmth. One way to add softness to a white room is to opt for white or cream with a lemon base. There are, however, other ways of adding warmth to a basically white color scheme. Using a warm color like peach or terracotta in tiling, flooring or furnishings, for example, would soften the room, but beware, as a large expanse of white with a minimal amount of these colors can look contrived and quite uneasy on the eye.

One of the most successful ways of bringing a mellow warmth to a white room is to use natural wood, which has a way of softening the hard edges of a color scheme. In this kitchen, the wood flooring, in particular, adds a casualness to a room that would have looked cold and unwelcoming if it had a more typical floor of white, gray or black ceramic or marble tiles.

LIGHTLY TOASTED
▼ The traditional toaster – with its enduring sense of style – has made a comeback and is the perfect design feature in a chrome kitchen.

w a r m   w o o d

The pattern in which the wood floor has been laid also has an effect on the appearance of the finished room. If the wood strips had been set to run the length of the kitchen through to the dining area, the floor would have looked longer, and the kitchen even narrower. If the strips had run horizontally, the room would have benefited from the appearance of extra width, but the lines of the kitchen might have appeared hard and square. The perfect solution was to run them diagonally, adding width and softer lines to the room.

COOL CHROME

▼ This kitchen looks extremely smart with its chrome appliances and accessories. Chrome has long been used in commercial settings because of its practical and hygienic qualities, and these have now been harnessed by designers to add a functional feel to domestic kitchens.

Clever color
combinations work

**COLOR
TECHNIQUES**
▲ Broken color effects
are popular
decorative techniques
that have been recently
revived. The method
creates "moving color"
and in the kitchen these
effects create a
scintillating scheme.

This kitchen is an excellent example of the new trend in interiors. It demonstrates a newfound confidence in the application of color and shows the ability of contemporary designers to blend a variety of textures and finishes successfully. A knowledge of the color wheel and color theory is invaluable here, as harnessing the power of color is integral to the success of this daringly finished room.

Emerald green cabinets, the central feature of this color scheme, nestle among a variety of colors, all of which contain a certain amount of red. Terracotta, pink and lavender are harmonious colors that sit to one side of the color wheel, and therefore naturally work well together when used in certain proportions. They also enhance the colors that they lie opposite, one of which is green, thereby explaining why these colors work together so successfully.

Many people find the bold use of color in this style of contemporary setting harsh. But the colorwashed finish on most of the painted walls in this room adds softness to the color scheme. This paint effect also acts as a textural link to the pale terracotta flooring, which might have appeared out of place if the room had been decorated using the same colors in their denser, more natural form.

To achieve this bold style of colorwashing, paint the wall surface with a pale-colored latex base

**STRIKING
BLIND**
▶ Many kitchens forego
curtains in favor of
more practical blinds.
In a daring color
scheme such as this,
opt for a striking blind
to pull all the color
elements together.

in harmony

coat and leave it to dry. Then water down your chosen decorative color. Use 1 part latex paint to 5 parts water. Working on one wall at a time, apply the paint with a 2-inch wide brush, moving the brush quickly in all directions. Occasionally stir the diluted paint mixture as the water and paint will begin to separate. As the paint dries, "paint" over the surface again, but without actually loading any more paint onto the brush. This will soften the initial paint marks.

LIGHT EFFECTS

▲ To make the best of a medley of colors you need to get the lighting just right. In the absence of natural light, use pure white halogen lighting, adding interest with spots and concealed lights.

Clever layout creates
a modern kitchen and

Large rooms like this one can be very effectively split into defined areas because of their generous proportions. It is not merely acceptable to use such a treatment in a large room, it is positively beneficial, as the overall effect can often be better when furniture is not just placed around the edges. This invariably leaves a large void in the center of the room, which can really only be filled with a dining table and chairs. Here, however, the units have been positioned to create a partition between the cooking area and the dining space. The cabinets in this run have varying heights to ensure the dining area remains integral to the main room while still offering maximum storage and working space. Because the partition runs from one wall and down through the center of the room, all services like electricity and water can be run from the outside wall and through the base cabinets. If these cabinets had been positioned as a central divider, with equal space for access on both sides, these essential services would have had to be run under the floor, or a step up onto a false floor.

COLOR COMBO
▼ This kitchen uses a great combination of easy-on-the-eye colors – off-white, green and honey brown.

The same principle applies to the "island" or central cooking unit, which does require a source of electricity to run under the floor. Always remember to account for supplies of water and power when planning the kitchen. If you are uncertain, ask the advice of a kitchen designer who will tell you what is practical, feasible and within your budget.

The splendid central island has a generous work space, which doubles as an additional, informal eating area. The room has a

dining area

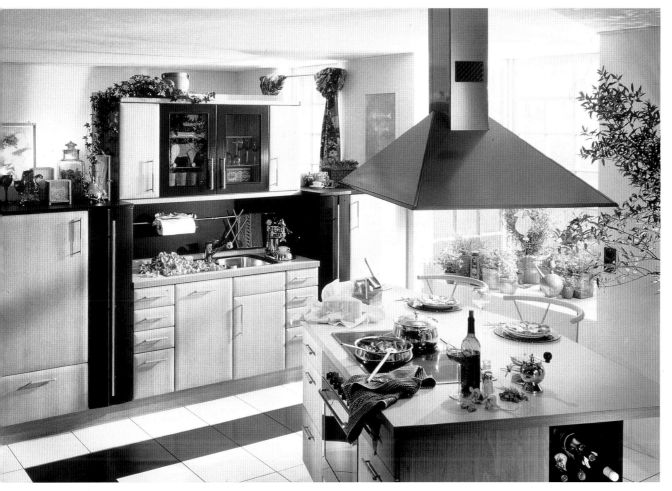

very mellow, yet contemporary feel to it. Off-white countertops team with natural alder wood in a gently curving design. A green contrast is incorporated in the side cabinets on the main run and in the pattern on the ceramic floor. These colors continue through to the dining area, where a golden, natural floor matting further enhances the division of space within the room. Finally, the room is well-coordinated using a mixture of natural wood, warm terracotta and an array of fresh green foliage. These final elements soften what could have been a rather clinical look and provide a pleasant aspect to a modern room.

TWO FROM ONE
▲ This smooth working kitchen is the essence of good design, where space has been maximized and two rooms have been created from one.

Cottage kitchens

COUNTRY HALLMARKS
▲ Antique pine and moss green woodwork are hallmarks of the country kitchen. The old-fashioned stoneware, range and marble-topped butcher's block contribute to the look.

To the traditionalists among us, the word "cottage" conjures up images of rustic wood, time-worn stone, quarry floors, and back-to-basics furnishings and cabinetry. To the more adventurous, however, the idea of the cottage interior offers the opportunity of creating a room with traditional cottage features mixed with more contemporary elements, complementary to a rural setting.

Regardless of their individual elements, cottage kitchens have a welcoming, unpretentious air. This is perpetuated by natural products and homespun fabrics. The last few years have seen a surge in the popularity of distressed painted furniture and rustic flooring; even modern paint finishes now emulate aged plaster walls. These contemporary elements are successfully used in the most modern of rooms. But because of their origins, they also work very well in a cottage environment. So it comes as no surprise to find a new wave of interiors incorporating these interpretations of traditional items.

The one thing they all have in common is their natural properties. The use of iron is the perfect example: this is a traditional product and has often been featured in the cottage kitchen as forged door hardware and cookstoves. Nowadays it is also the material for contemporary dining furniture and accessories. Likewise, there has been a resurgence in natural paints such as distemper and limewash, which bring greater authenticity to today's cottage kitchen.

PAINT EFFECTS

▼ Contemporary elements like modern paint techniques and painted furniture in modern colors sit perfectly in this cottage kitchen. The overwhelming feeling is one of traditional quality and natural rustic charm.

OLD BEAMS

◀ Exposed beams make an architectural statement in a cottage kitchen. New faux beams can give the illusion of a traditional form of construction inside the most modern properties.

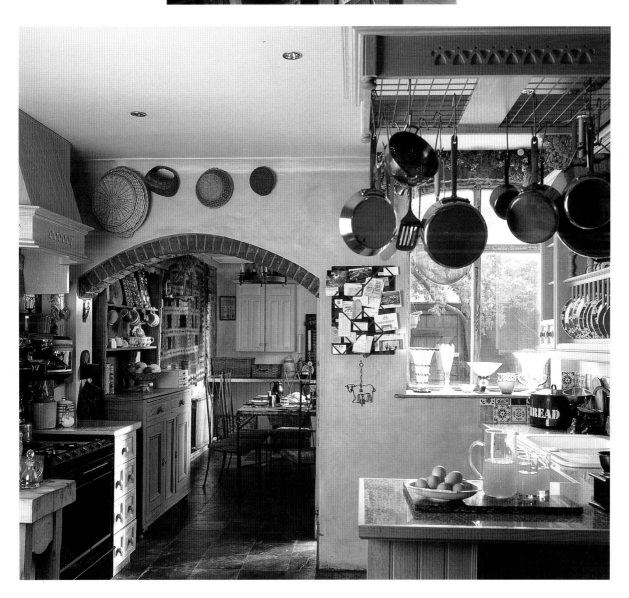

Old-fashioned kitchenware
provides a

Pine is one of the woods most often associated with the cottage interior, and there is a wide assortment of pine furniture available. Although the revival of interest in pine furniture over the past decade or so has made it harder to find reasonably priced antiques, there are now a number of manufacturers using traditional methods to produce excellent pieces of furniture from reclaimed timber. These make a perfectly acceptable substitute, while having the benefit of being available to order in any shape and size imaginable. This makes the job of creating a practical and authentic- looking cottage kitchen ever simpler.

Originally, only freestanding pieces of furniture would have been found in a cottage kitchen, but nowadays a careful blend of both built-in and freestanding pieces can fulfill the needs of the modern family without straying too far from a traditional style of decor. The back-to-basics feel of a traditional cottage can also be retained by concealing modern appliances behind cabinet fronts.

The cooking range is a dominant feature in the traditional cottage kitchen. There are now a number of traditionally styled ranges available, inspired by the popularity of solid fuel and gas-powered enameled ranges. Originally, the range was both a reliable cooking appliance and a source of heat for the home. The new wave of gas and electric ranges, however, are purely for cooking. The positioning of the traditional enameled range was once restricted because they needed to be vented and therefore would have to be placed close

FINISHING TOUCHES
▼ Old-fashioned enameled tinware and china can be bought quite inexpensively to complete the country look.

homely look

NOSTALGIC ACCESSORIES

◀ Traditional accessories and clutter are all part of the character associated with a cottage-style kitchen. No matter how confined the space – and country kitchens by their very nature are small – be sure to have a good mix of china, enameled tinware and nostalgic paraphernalia.

CHECK OUT

▼ Checked fabrics have long been associated with country-style decor. Use them to make simple curtains and valances for the windows, or to cover unsightly areas that lurk below the sink.

to an outside wall. Today, power flues can be used to draw the fumes a greater distance, giving modern kitchen designers more flexibility when planning.

The kitchen featured here not only uses traditional products such as the cookstove and the cast-iron sink, but it also uses traditional colors to evoke the nostalgia of an old-fashioned cottage kitchen. Buttermilk walls give the room a warmth reminiscent of age-stained paintwork, while deep bottle green adds depth and definition to the color scheme.

Solid oak kitchen given a
country touch with fabric

As with all interior design styles there are many interpretations of an original look. These normally incorporate up-to-date features and products designed to make maintenance as simple as possible, enabling the room to include the best of modern design within a traditional atmosphere.

The kitchen featured here is manufactured from solid oak, a material traditionally associated with country kitchens. The decorator has decided to enhance its traditional qualities further by covering the kitchen walls with a pretty floral stripe wallpaper, setting the table with a patchwork-printed fabric as a contrast

TRADITIONAL DETAILING

▼ The traditional cottage kitchen features freestanding items of furniture, which do not always fulfill the needs of the modern family. A modern kitchen incorporating traditional details and dressed with cottage-style furnishings may be the perfect solution.

and flowers

and dressing the windows with checked curtains. The same checked fabric has been used for the frilled and deep-buttoned seat cushions tied with generous bows to the back of each chair. These, together with the accessories and details like the dried flowers displayed above the wall units, create a modern kitchen with a distinctly rural feel.

This cottage kitchen is fully appointed with built-in cabinets and therefore offers ample storage and concealed appliances, features that give the family a practical working environment. A deep drawer next to the oven is an excellent feature that is now incorporated into many kitchens, as pots and pans can be stacked and retrieved more easily from here than from the back of a cabinet.

The countertops are covered in ceramic tiles that continue up the wall, creating a hygienic, easily cleaned surface. Care must be taken, however, if using ceramics on countertop surfaces as some glazes may be susceptible to staining. Also, always use the correct adhesives and grouts to ensure impervious joints where no bacteria can grow.

The floor tiles provide an interesting variation on the cottage hearth rug. A checkerboard pattern has been created in the center of the floor. This has the effect of breaking up what could otherwise be a large expanse of cream tiles. It also makes the dining area look more homey. The choice of colors links in with the work surface tiles and checked curtains, and the cream wallpaper.

FINISHING TOUCH
▲ Swags of dried flowers are the perfect country accessory for a kitchen such as this.

SOFT DETAILS
▼ Look in any fabric store and you will find a wide variety of checked and floral fabrics from which you can make cushion covers, table-cloths and curtains for a country-style kitchen.

Rustic brick and wood –
the ultimate

Nearly two decades ago, a leading kitchen design house introduced a simple, country, handmade pine kitchen and it took the industry by storm. Its continued popularity has made this style of kitchen a design classic. Traditional paneled doors, pine knobs and fretwork are all important features of this style of country kitchen. Other features that recall the simple cottage style are the plate drainage racks above the sink area, small drawers for storing all those bits and pieces that always seem to amass in the kitchen, and cabinet doors with glass panels.

Rustic timbers feature heavily in the design of this kitchen, both as beams on the ceiling and as supporting upright posts, giving the kitchen an authentic appearance. If your kitchen is not of this period, introducing fake timbers can set the scene.

A flagstone floor is both practical and beautiful, and in this case it blends with the exposed rustic brickwork. There is a wide range of flooring tiles available and if you can't afford the expense of original stone tiles, vinyl flooring is a good imitation – and it is warmer underfoot, too. If you want to use brick in your kitchen, as here, secondhand bricks are best for this setting as their mellow tones complement the woodwork and their slightly crumbled edges have a worn softness not found in modern bricks.

Above the food preparation area an old-fashioned drying rack holds saucepans and cookware. It is both practical and a charming decorative feature.

BRICK CLADDING

▲ Rustic brick and traditional blue and white china are key elements in the country-style kitchen. If you are unable to expose natural brickwork, modern brick cladding is actually a very realistic alternative.

country kitchen

Finally, there is a traditional cooking range, housed in a brick arched recess, that is reminiscent of the inglenook fireplaces of years gone by. This traditional cooking appliance is the main feature of the kitchen, emphasizing the fact that the cottage kitchen represents the heart of the home, where the family gathers by the warmth of the range to be fed good, hearty, home-produced meals. Today's ranges are available in a far greater number of colors than in years gone by, making them traditional and yet also contemporary in their feel.

COPPER
▲ An authentic touch – antique copper saucepans hanging from the wall or an overhead rack. Buy reproduction pans if you can't get originals.

BARLEY TWIST
▼ The attractive scrolls running up each of the units draw together the disparate elements in this kitchen.

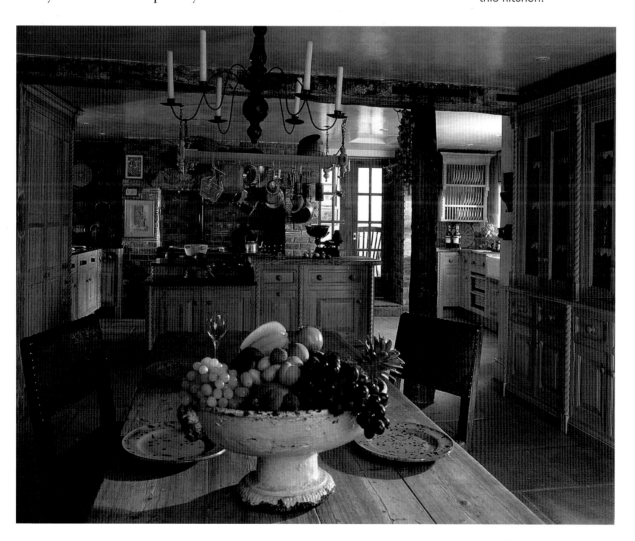

Family kitchens

In terms of decoration, family kitchens can fall into any design category, but at the planning stage, additional time and thought

must be given to ensuring that the family kitchen fulfills the needs of each person. Safety is of utmost importance, and the design should be practical, too, offering adequate storage, cooking and working facilities. The working area will often extend beyond the preparation of food, as this is quite likely the place where children play or study under a parent's watchful eye.

A ROOM TO ENJOY

▲ This splendid kitchen is clearly the hub of the family home. It is used for both social and practical purposes.

The best way to tackle the planning is to note the primary functions of the finished room. List them in order of priority and the available space can then be allocated suitably, to create a room specially tailored to the needs of your family.

When choosing products for a family kitchen, select them with care as the room will suffer more wear than that used by a retired couple, for example. It is important to strike a balance between the practical and the aesthetic, too. All surfaces should be easy to clean and maintain in a family kitchen. If you have a young family, there is a wide range of kitchen safety equipment available, covering everything from door locks for your cabinets to safety guards for the cooktop. These are essential for a safe environment, and once your family has grown, they can all be removed. Safety does not have to be at the expense of style – good planning can supply both.

GENEROUS PROPORTIONS

⬒ This kitchen has a generous dining/ working area that is ideal for both family gatherings and the quieter moments when the children need time to concentrate and study within earshot of a parent.

GOOD PLANNING

◀ This galley kitchen may not offer a large dining or play area, but the space available has been used to produce an efficient kitchen equipped to service the needs of a growing family. Cooking, food storage and laundry requirements are all provided for.

Old-world charm
for relaxed

This authentic rural kitchen is undoubtedly unique in its origin, but its charm and simplicity would be easy to replicate for anyone eager to create a similar look in their home.

The flooring is traditional slate slabs, which have the advantage of being extremely hard wearing, although a little chilly underfoot. This type of flooring is now widely available, in a number of color variations. If you like the look of stone but slate doesn't fit into your color scheme, consider large ceramic tiles that mimic the look of stone. Granite tiles, which come in a variety of colors, are also an attractive and durable option.

NOSTALGIA
▼ Recreating a family room like this would not be difficult: it contains a carefree
mix of inexpensive items acquired over the years.

family gatherings

The walls have been painted with a pale blue oil-based paint that is easy to wipe clean, hard-wearing and gives a soft sheen to the walls. It is also of a type that adheres to both timber and plaster work, enabling the wooden partition to be painted with the same product. This wall houses the stairs leading to the upper floor, and while in modern houses it would be constructed from either blocks and plaster or timber and plasterboard, the original wood planks are on display here adding to the atmosphere of the room. This could easily be copied using tongue-and-groove paneling in the modern kitchen.

The generous cooking range is original, but due to its time-less appeal, is of a type still manufactured today. There are also modern ranges available that are designed to look like the traditional range, but incorporate modern features and energy efficiency.

While the range is undoubtedly the most impor-tant item in this kitchen, the dining table and chairs are the core around which life in the kitchen revolves. This table is served by six raffia ladder-back chairs and one pine one. The mixture of two paint colors and natural wood adds to the relaxed atmosphere, a trick that can easily be copied.

THE RANGE

◁ Ranges like this are manufactured in a wider choice of colors than used to be the case. They are the perfect form of stove for the family kitchen, and can be purchased inexpen-sively as well.

FLOOR COVERINGS

▽ Oriental rugs need not be expensive; a great many passable imitations are made that would add color and warmth to a kitchen with hard stone flooring.

Vivid colors
add vibrancy to

Most families need to find a great deal of space for the many time-saving devices now available, such as microwave ovens, food processors, juicers, or even coffee makers. A kitchen with a full array of cabinets is the best solution for people who need generous amounts of storage, unless the house has a traditional pantry space. One of the other benefits of kitchen cabinets is that they are available in a wide range of styles and finishes, most of which have been designed and manufactured to offer the best in storage and easy cleaning and maintenance. This kitchen offers all these benefits, with the addition of a bright, fun and safe environment for the whole family.

The oven is housed within a wall unit ensuring it is out of the reach of the children and also at a level that is easily accessible. Directly above the oven there is a small built-in microwave oven behind a cabinet panel, again out of the children's reach and hidden from view, keeping the kitchen as streamlined as possible. The cooktop is surrounded by a removable chrome safety guard – a vital safety device to prevent a curious toddler from pulling down a burning pot on his or her head. The controls to the cooktop are sited above it rather than underneath. This clever positioning keeps the controls away from children's ever-inquisitive fingers but at a perfect height for an adult.

In a well-designed kitchen such as this, all other appliances such as the refrigerator, freezer and dishwasher can be installed

soft background tones

FAMILY PLANNING

◀ This kitchen in light beech and pale green has been specifically planned for a growing family, offering safety features and a stream-lined, ergonomic layout to make it pleasant to work in while providing plenty of floor and tabletop space.

behind cabinet panels, in the same way as the microwave. The kitchen remains neat and the appliances hidden.

Decoratively, the light green and pale beech cabinets are the perfect simple backdrop to the brightly colored accessories that have been chosen to enhance the room. When decorating any room that will regularly house children, do not forget to allow space for all their colorful toys and accessories.

BRIGHT LIGHTS

▼ Vivid colors in modern, translucent plastic or glass light up a primarily neutral kitchen.

A contemporary edge to
a traditional kitchen

Having the confidence to mix different styles purely because you like them is a wonderful attribute. It is normally only through trial and error that you can discover if contrasting ideas will work, and if you like them and can live with them in your home, it is the perfect opportunity to run with your instinct.

Sometimes it is very difficult to analyze rooms where different looks have been used successfully together. For example, this mixture of contemporary black and cream furnishings with traditional pine may only work well because of the balance that has been created in the room. The basic kitchen has been framed by modern wallpaper and a border, while the tablecloth echoes their color and design, drawing them into the center of the room.

A few days ago, a friend who is decorating her kitchen asked for my advice. She had chosen a dark oak traditional kitchen and was pondering on her next design decision as the cabinets would fit in well with either one of two styles. Should she give the room a country atmosphere? She favors and has lived successfully with this style for many years, but she also wondered if she should take a more formal approach, making the room more like that in a town house. Her choice would determine whether the ceiling should be accented with wood beams or whether a decorative cove molding should be installed.

As she is very familiar with my own method of decorating, and was well aware of my love of rooms in which styles are blended, she also considered using both approaches in her room. In theory, this sounds a good compromise, but if you are adding architectural details, it is important they favor only one style so that the room remains intrinsically whole. In this case, rustic beams would look completely out of character with the room if an ornate coving were also to be used. My advice was to decide on which look she wanted to establish as the room's central theme, and then if she wanted to add some contrast, she could do this with the interior decor and accessories.

BALANCING ACT

▼ Combining traditional cabinets with contemporary decor can work well as long as the correct balance is made. Here the wallpaper surrounds the kitchen and the eye is drawn into the center by the boldly patterned tablecloth.

Country & town house

The country and town house styles of decorating fall somewhere between grand and rustic. Traditionally, many country house

owners also had a house in the town, which is where the crossover of style originates. The owners were more prosperous than their country cottage neighbors, so the furniture and furnishings purchased for such houses was grander, yet subject to the decorative trends of the day, while still blending in perfectly with a country style, such as full-blown rose chintz fabrics used for soft furnishings and curtaining.

PERIOD STYLE
▲ Reproduction antique French-style dining chairs grace the dining table in this kitchen. Note how well they blend with traditional practical elements like the plate rack and simple wall-mounted shelves.

The country house kitchen originally offered the occupant the best design that money could buy, but in a distinctly more casual style than that of the town house. Many of the larger country houses had lavishly equipped kitchens with walls of built-in storage and generously sized stoves. This is where the traditional kitchen cabinets originated, either in natural wood or painted, as is typical of many turn-of-the-century houses. They were designed for a working environment – to be practical, with hard-wearing stone or quarry tiled floors, and large pine or scrubbed oak tables. These are elements that can still be seen in the country house style kitchen, but as these rooms are not only for the use of food preparation, they may be blended with the grander furniture found in other rooms.

TRADITIONAL PAINTS

▼ Painted traditional kitchen cabinets have a more formal appearance than their pine or oak alternatives, ideal for reproducing this style of kitchen.

COUNTRY HOUSE DETAILS

◀ Traditional rural features like rustic flooring, pressed tiles and wicker are teamed with a smart painted kitchen to produce a more formal country house style.

Making the most of
light and space

What style of kitchen would you have if you blended hand-crafted traditional pine cabinets, a smart terracotta and ceramic floor and a stunning conservatory? Well, you would have a unique room that combines rustic charm with the elegance that comes from a large, traditional glass extension.

The expanses of glass makes this room look quite light and airy. However, the kitchen does not lack privacy even though the generous sash window has no curtaining. Instead, the lower two

TILE FLOORING
▶ The terracotta and textured ceramic floor combines the rustic qualities associated with terracotta and quarry tiles with the easy maintenance of a glazed ceramic tile. It also adds a block of pattern to the large floor area, reducing its apparent size and making it seem less daunting.

panes have been decorated with glass paints to obscure vision into the room. These paints are available at various craft outlets and by mail order. Although they require a little practice, using the paints is not beyond the talents of most of us, and they are effective in providing privacy without cutting out too much light.

Attention to detail is very important in this room. Note the room divider, for example. It has been made from the same wood as the main kitchen units and makes a definite "partition" between the main food preparation area and the dining space. The open shelves on the divider are used as a display area and there are also compartments designed to hold cutlery.

The countertops are tiled to offer a hard-wearing, practical and aesthetically pleasing surface. The white ceramic tiles continue up the wall to provide a backsplash area around the sink. A white and terracotta border has been incorporated to add pattern to the walls and to draw the floor colors up and around the

window. The border has been finished off with narrow wooden beading, creating a neat edge to the tiles. There are a number of solutions to finishing a ceramic tiled wall, including the beading used here, or plastic trims that sit behind the tile and create a rounded edge. Alternatively, look for traditional rounded tiles, available in some ceramic tile stores.

Casual elegance for
a kitchen/family room

DECORATIVE MOLDINGS

▼ Architectural devices such as moldings, architraves and cornices were pivotal design elements of the townhouse room. They are available in a variety of patterns and can be painted or stained as you wish.

The priority in this beautiful room is undoubtedly comfort and not the need for a large cooking and preparation area. However, you can still achieve a great deal in a small but well-planned kitchen. The room is split into different working areas that aesthetically combine to produce one large, pleasing room. The arched stone recess houses the stove, low-level storage units and some discreet shelves on each side of the worktop, creating a compact space for food preparation. The more traditional approach to an area like this one would have been to install a larger range, as may have originally been placed there. But in a room where space is at a premium it is better to include storage space as well.

Central to this arrangement is the oak table, providing a pleasant dining space as well as an extra work surface. To its right are the sink, dishwasher and refrigerator which have all been housed discreetly in buttermilk-painted cabinets. These are the same color as the walls to ensure the kitchen is as unobtrusive as possible, once again enhancing the feeling that the room is primarily one in which to relax.

The wonderful wood floor and stone-clad arch decorated with a pair of antlers add a country feel to the room so that it is somewhat reminiscent of a traditional hunting lodge. But the approach to the rest of the decor is less rustic. A breakfront glazed cabinet houses a collection of traditional china and glass, to the side of which nestles a comfortable down-filled sofa. The sofa sports blue scatter cushions and there is some blue china on the coffee table. These are interesting additions as blue is a color not used elsewhere in the room; instead, the majority of the scheme is made up of sunny creams and green. But the blue acts to add both a contrast of color and to create a more informal mood in the room.

Finally, the room is completed with a well-chosen range of accessories. Note the informal collection of cards positioned on the wall above the sink. Each one is framed using a simple glass clip frame, which creates a cost-effective and casual display.

COMPACT KITCHEN

▲ The cooking area of the kitchen is truly compact. Bulky saucepans, colanders and sieves are left to hang rather than fill the small cupboards, and shelves are tucked into the recesses behind the stone arch.

Old-fashioned virtues combir
with modern practicality

This beautiful painted kitchen looks as though it has evolved lovingly over a period of years. Instead, it is an excellent example of a contemporary painted kitchen that incorporates both traditional and modern features. For example, the square paneling and inset drawer fronts – teamed with details like the plate rack and free-standing dresser – are in the traditional mode. However, there are also elements of the built-in kitchen (the countertops and range hood) that, together with contemporary paint techniques and colors, create an overall effect that is far from rustic.

Generally, the room has the feel of a totally freestanding kitchen, even though the majority of the cabinets are built in. This is achieved by keeping the run of countertops and base cabinets to a minimum. Breaks in continuity, however small, create groups of cabinets that act like selected individual pieces. For example, the housing for the extractor fan is attached to two small side cabinets, whereas the plate rack is separated from its adjacent unit. Varying surface levels has the same effect, and adds extra interest to the layout. The ceramic tiles, too, are kept to a block around the cooking area, as opposed to running along the length of the countertops, as is more usual.

When you look at the pieces in detail, both the dresser and the main working area include identical design details – even the same handles. But by changing the color of the units,

DETAILS, DETAILS

▼ Yellow and blue complement each other so beautifully that in a kitchen that features mellow wooden and wicker baskets, blue paint and furnishings provide the perfect backdrop.

the effect is that of individual pieces of furniture, with different characters. This helps the kitchen to appear as if it has developed gradually rather than been clinically manufactured. The dresser does not look isolated, however, as the blue color is cleverly echoed in the cabinet linings on the open units and also features in the ceramic tiles.

A quick and simple way to alter the feel of a kitchen is by changing the drawer and door knobs. These usually screw in and out very easily. Imagine how this kitchen would look if the knobs were much larger, or were made of brass or ceramic.

COMPLETING THE LOOK

▲ The room has a calm, slightly mellow feel due to the chosen flooring: stone, featuring flashes of warm peach and charcoal colors.

Soft milky creams
brightened with

This town house kitchen/dining room offers the best of smart family living. The functional kitchen is divided into two areas: the main food preparation area, which is accessed via the white paneled double doors, and the cooking and dining space in the well-proportioned main room. This is an interesting division as the cooking space would normally be positioned in the main preparation area, but informal dining can leave the chef in front of the stove while guests or family gather by the table. So why not place them together? This layout also means that any mess created when preparing the meal can still be well hidden behind the double doors.

The design of the cabinets in the main room takes advantage of the room's high ceilings and the striking proportions. The stove is housed within a classical-style layout with a tiled back panel and recessed paneled door cabinets, which offer ample storage. This is finished with routed columns and a classical pediment at the top. The columns protrude from the base and outer side cabinets, creating an interesting break at the front of what would otherwise have been a plain bank of cabinets.

The double oven is housed in the side cabinets to the left of the cooktop. This is counter-balanced by the tall cabinet with the same proportions on the opposite side – a layout that is fundamental to the overall appearance of the kitchen.

In essence, this kitchen has a very formal air, but the natural wood floor and plain wood table add a

**PLAIDS
PROVIDE FLAIR**
▼ Bright, modern plaids and large checks add flair to an otherwise plain or neutral room. Ivory, cream and natural terracotta provide the perfect foil for these strong but harmonious colors.

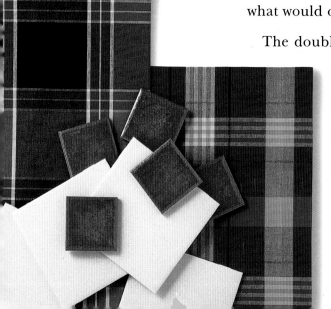

modern plaid

more approachable feel. When this is teamed with the ample storage offered by this kitchen it creates a welcoming environment for a family, with plenty of room for the hustle and bustle of normal family life. At the same time, it is perfectly styled for urban living.

STRIKING ARCHITECTURE
▼ Strong architectural details are enhanced in this town house kitchen. By keeping the colors muted, fabrics can afford to be bold.

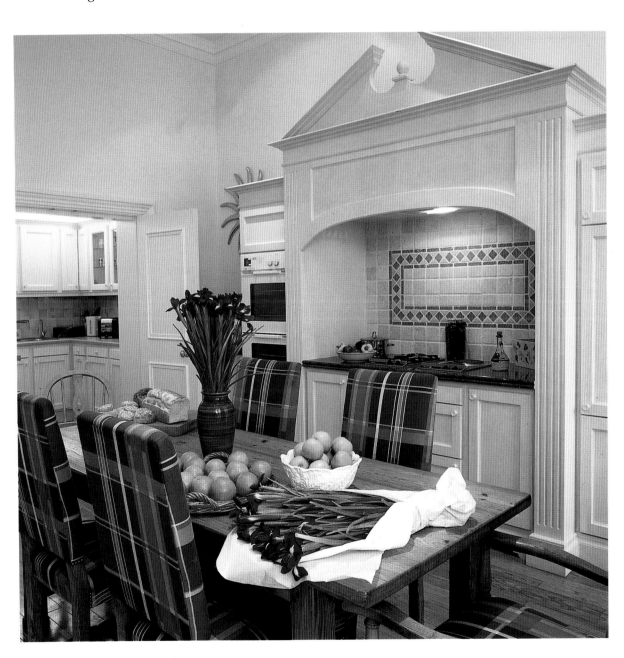

FOCUS *file*

You will now be very familiar with the various styles of kitchen that are available, and if you are planning to replace or upgrade your own kitchen you have hopefully come a long way towards

making a decision about the style you would like in your home. The rooms featured in the Style File chapter on pages 10-59 will have given you a wide range of ideas and you will be able to determine why these rooms work so successfully, but there is still a large amount of information to help you make wise choices when selecting the principal elements that will make up your dream kitchen.

Over the next few pages, we examine the various peripheral products on the market from which you can make these all-important choices.

Sinks and countertops take a great deal of wear and tear in a kitchen, so some background information on what is available will help you make the right decision. Technology has played a large role in developing materials that are ideal for the kitchen environment, having the beauty of traditional materials but the durability only space-age science can produce. We also look at the types of flooring and wallcoverings that are most suitable for a kitchen – those that withstand stains, steam, condensation and grease – together with information on lighting and window treatments.

It is a good idea to read all the sections within Focus File, especially if you are still unsure about the final look you want to achieve. There may be one item that really catches your imagination – a stone sink, or a tiled work surface – or you may discover that a specific type of product may be more practical in your situation, making a decision easier to reach. Don't feel daunted, just enjoy the pleasure of making those decisions.

SHOP AROUND
▼ The choice is astonishing, so shop around, mix and match, and plan carefully to get the best kitchen for you.

Walls *and* floors

Wall and floor finishes need especially careful consideration in the kitchen as it is the one room in the home that is subjected to hard wear, vigorous cleaning and constant variations in temperature and humidity. This means that a fine balance must be met when choosing these finishes, weighing practical considerations with aesthetic preferences.

If you are thinking of using wallpaper, then solid vinyl is an excellent option, as it has a thick polymer coating that acts as a barrier to water penetration. Wallpaper is best avoided in areas subjected to constant steam or cleaning, however, as their color and coating will eventually wear away, so areas such as behind the stove and sink are best covered in a more robust product like paint, plastic or tiles.

Paints are a good option for the kitchen, and manufacturers now produce mildew and moisture-resistant products especially for the kitchen and bathroom. Paints with an eggshell or vinyl finish are perfect, but if you like the sheen of high gloss, make sure you have adequate ventilation, as this can worsen condensation problems.

Graining, colorwashing, distressing and stenciling are now all part of the home decorator's list of achievable finishes. A great number of magazines and books are available that explain exactly how to recreate these effects if you are unsure.

It is also becoming increasingly popular to use

CLEAR LIGHT
▼ The glass blocks used in this kitchen act as both a construction material and a decorative finish, giving the room light and vitality.

RUSTIC TILES
◀ ▼ Hand-decorated ceramic and terracotta tiles from all parts of the world are now readily available to the home decorator. They add an individual touch that cannot be emulated by any other product.

water-based paints on all surfaces in the kitchen to make color matching easier. In such cases, protect the woodwork with a coat or two of acrylic varnish. This is especially worthwhile on distressed paint finishes.

Many color schemes include stained and painted wood – either in natural tones or more colorful washes – for both walls and floors. And with a quality varnish and sealant over the top, most woods can now be used in areas such as the sink without danger of warping or distortion.

Ceramic, marble and quarry tiles offer a very versatile and practical finish for both walls and floors in a kitchen. These natural products will withstand a great deal of wear and are available in practically every color, pattern and style imaginable.

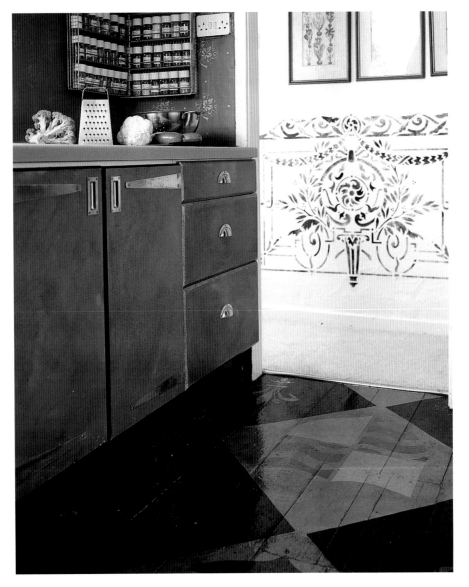

**PAINTERLY
DETAILS**
◀ Here, paint finishes
have been used to
decorate both walls and
floor. The wood floor
has been painted and
stenciled, while a more
fanciful stencil has
been applied to the
plain white walls. A
metallic paint effect
gives the backsplashes
and kitchen cabinets
added interest.

Ceramic tiles are particularly varied and can be laid in patterns of your own choice. Consider combining different colors of the same hand-painted motif, using molded chair rails or picture tiles among plain white tiles. If you are planning on using tiles as a backsplash, take advantage of the modern adhesives and grouts now available as they team with the product to create a bacteria-free and hard-wearing surface.

For the floor, in addition to ceramic tiles, there is also a wonderful selection of slate, terracotta and stone, all of which are extremely hard-wearing. These products have a unique quality and style, but will need more maintenance than other types of hard flooring if they are to avoid greasy stains becoming permanent. They are also expensive options, will definitely need installation by an expert, are hard underfoot, and any dropped dishes will undoubtedly break on such a surface, so keep these points in mind when making your choice.

Softer floorings include natural wood, cork tiles and vinyl, which together offer an extensive palette of colors and designs for your kitchen. If you are laying cork or vinyl, it is best to prepare the bare floor first to provide a sound base. Do this by laying small sheets of hardboard (soak them first and lay them rough side up) securing them with ring nails, which have more of a grip than ordinary nails.

Vinyl is a cheaper and warmer alternative to hard tiles and there are many very passable imitations available both as tiles and sheet flooring. The disadvantage of using wood or vinyl is the fact that water can penetrate to the floor below. So if any of your appliances were to overflow or leak, you could end up with problems. You should therefore choose these types of product with care.

FINISHING TOUCHES
▲ Ceramic tiles now incorporate every style of decoration imaginable. This little badger would bring a smile to your face on the busiest of days.

HARD WEARING
▼ Small tile insets between larger floor tiles break up a surface and give it added interest.

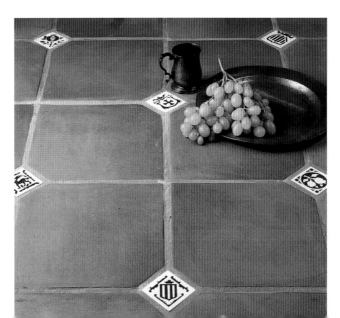

Work surfaces *and* sinks

Two of the main areas in your kitchen that will take most of the wear and tear are the sink and countertop areas. There is now an extremely large choice of products available to fulfill both the practical requirements of a busy kitchen and your aesthetic needs to enhance your chosen style of decor.

In the traditional kitchen, natural finishes and products with conventional origins obviously work best. Wooden countertops can be used throughout or can be used alongside ceramic tiled surfaces in country or traditional styles. But choose wooden countertops with care as not all woods are suitable (hardwood is best), and all will require a certain amount of maintenance in the form of oiling or waxing to keep the wood waterproof and looking its best.

VERSATILE TILES

▼ Don't restrict ceramic tiles to walls and floors – they make perfect work surfaces, providing you choose ones specifically designed for the purpose.

Ceramic tiles come in a very wide range of styles and designs and they look at home in all settings, not just traditional interiors. Sadly, many people have been put off using ceramics for worktops because of problems encountered in the past. For example, thin wall tiles are not substantial enough to withstand the possible impact from heavy pots and pans and any work surface fitted with these is likely to crack. Fortunately, there are many more suitable tiles, but make sure that you choose a tile with a glaze that will not discolor. Likewise, grout used to be rather unstable, but all this is in the past now. Modern technology has supplied us with epoxy adhesives and grouts which, when used correctly, create a surface that is impervious to germs and dirt.

Granite is another increasingly popular alternative for work surfaces, offering a variety of color choices. Granite can make a very serviceable worktop, as it is both hard-wearing and easy to clean. If you choose to use either granite or marble, it should be cut and installed by an expert and allowances made for a variation of color between each sheet – after all, this is a natural product.

Modern products, such as laminates and Corian, in finishes that emulate the above products, also have their place in the traditional kitchen. These can have the same overall effect on the design of your room as the original, with the added benefit of the advantages that come from modern technology. In many

TWO-TONE
◀ The modern sink is available in almost any color and style imaginable. Here, the two-tone colorway adds an interesting feature.

TONING-IN
▲ A laminated worktop with a wooden edge that matches the rest of the kitchen acts as a housing for a small, well-designed white enameled sink.

PRACTICAL FEATURES
▲ A modern sink unit with a deep bowl and high rim prevents water from splashing onto the neighboring countertop. The sliding cutting board is a useful feature.

SHINING SURFACES
▼ As people take home entertaining and food preparation more seriously, products traditionally used in the professional kitchen are now being used in a domestic setting.

cases, these products can, in fact, be more cost effective that the natural finishes that are available.

Choosing contemporary countertops for the kitchen can be difficult as manufacturers now produce every shade and finish of laminate imaginable. In addition, products like Corian can be cast in any color and shape to form worktops that incorporate sink and dish drainer areas. These finishes also have the benefit of being nonporous, and, as they are solid, can be sanded and polished to remove any blemishes and burns that may occur over time.

Used less now for countertops are thin laminate veneers, which are bonded to a base of either chipboard or plywood. These finishes are serviceable and easy to clean, but they should not be used as cutting or chopping surfaces, as a knife will penetrate them, creating a weak spot through which moisture can penetrate, possibly causing the wood below to swell and distort.

Chrome, a product traditionally associated with the professional kitchen and once reserved just for the sink, has now become widely used in the domestic setting as a hard-wearing worktop, backsplash, range hood or storage.

Clay and stone sinks look wonderful in a truly traditional setting, but are quite difficult to obtain. A good alternative is the practical cast-iron – or butler's – sink, which has grown in popularity recently and is also easily available, offering a substantial washing facility for the traditional kitchen. There are

OLD STYLE

◀ This old stone sink and wall-mounted faucets look wonderful in a traditional setting, but they can be hard to obtain. If you have your heart set on one, contact your local stone mason to see if a sink can be made specially for you.

also a number of companies specializing in ceramic, brass and enamelware, all of which can create an eye-catching feature within the kitchen.

Kitchen and appliance designers are now spending as much time on the design and development of the domestic sink and dish drainer as they do a piece of art. There are also literally thousands of faucet options, to complement any decor. Finally, keep in mind the functions of your sink area, as you are no longer restricted to a bowl and drain board. Look for single and double drain boards, half and single bowls, integrated chopping boards, inset draining racks and waste disposal units.

Storage *ideas*

Many people make the mistake of thinking that the more cabinets you have in the kitchen, the better. While it may be true to say that you can never have too many well-designed storage units, efficient organization of the contents of your kitchen offers a better solution. Cabinets need not only be at ground level, nor need they all be of the same height. Cabinets attached to walls at eye-level height make good use of what can often be wasted space. They are also especially useful for storing items that need to be kept away from children's sticky fingers or, if you have glass-fronted doors, for displaying favorite pieces of china or dinnerware. If there is space, a large cupboard that reaches

ALL STORED AWAY

▼ Cabinets and drawers come in a wide variety of shapes and sizes which is just what is needed to make the most of storing the contents of a kitchen.

to the ceiling will provide splendid opportunities for storage.

Open plate racks or shelves are the perfect home for everyday china, and again add decorative detail to the room while supplying storage that is easily accessible. Position such storage racks within easy reach of the dishwasher or sink to save time and breakage.

For those who have moved into an older house in which there is a pantry, please think twice before having it removed. Unless the kitchen is extremely small, the traditional shelved, walk-in pantry can house far more than the best kitchen cabinet layout. Originally, the pantry would have been situated on an outside wall with good ventilation and this – coupled with a stone floor – would have created a cool, airy space. Today, despite central heating, pantries are still surprisingly efficient at keeping food and wine cool. In fact, many kitchen designers are now incorporating large floor-to-ceiling pantry or larder cupboards to replace the originals.

Modern designs of kitchen offer many storage solutions, such as fold-away ironing boards, pull-out trash bins and tables, and waste disposal units to keep the kitchen as streamlined as possible. Drawers of varying sizes are especially useful for storing different sized items. Small drawers are great for cutlery and dish towels, say, while deep drawers make it easy to store larger items like casserole dishes and stacks of plates. Estimate your requirements and then choose your cabinets accordingly.

HANG-UPS
◀ Saucepans and other kitchen utensils can be decorative so hang them up as a display and use the cabinets for other, less attractive kitchenware.

SMALL SPACES
▼ If you have room to stow a large refrigerator elsewhere, keep a small one in the kitchen for everyday items.

NOVEL STORES
▲ A mixture of storage in a contemporary, Shaker style. The peg board is set around the whole room and is perfect for hanging almost anything; the wicker drawers not only look good but also provide excellent storage for fruit and vegetables. And note the useful and decorative plate rack.

WASTED SPACE
▶ These attractive wall units, designed in Art Deco style, provide storage with flair. Remember that wall cabinets make good use of areas that would otherwise be wasted.

Unless totally custom, even the modern kitchen will have the odd space where the smallest standard cabinet is too large to fit. Ask a carpenter to help you adapt these spaces to house thin baking tins or chopping boards, and consider replacing the panels at the bottom of your kitchen base cabinets with custom-made drawers to store linen or baking equipment. All too often it is these last pieces of equipment with their awkward shapes that clutter full-size cabinets.

If you have the advantage of a separate utility room, use it to house a large refrigerator or freezer, and fit a small integrated larder refrigerator, which will take up minimum space, in the kitchen. This can house the items that you most regularly use such as milk, butter and cheese, while larger items can be stored elsewhere until needed.

Be ruthless when it comes to organizing the contents of your kitchen. If something is used less than once a week it should not take up prime-access storage space. Conversely, condiments, herbs, spices and oils used regularly in cooking should be kept near the stove and easily accessible. Cooking pots and pans should be within easy reach, too, and can even add atmosphere to a room if displayed within view. This then frees up valuable cabinet space for other, less attractive, items, or items that are used less frequently.

The kitchen with good storage has a mixture of built-in and open storage that has been carefully planned. This, combined with the good positioning of the contents of your kitchen, will offer you the best in storage solutions.

MAKING THE MOST OF IT
▲ A well-planned kitchen has plenty of storage space. Mix glass-fronted cupboards with those that conceal appliances and unattractive cookware.

Window *treatments*

SIMPLE TIES

▼ Simple, unlined curtains such as these can be quickly removed and laundered – a necessity in a steamy kitchen. Ties in a contrast fabric, rather than more formal hooks, are used to hang the curtains on the rod.

Unless your kitchen is very grand or incorporates a formal dining area, the secret to successful kitchen window treatments lies in simplicity. Because kitchen curtains need more regular laundering than those in any other room in the home, they should be simple to remove, re-attach and dress, and preferably be made from easily washable fabrics. Be aware, however, that most lined curtains should, where possible, be dry cleaned as even if the main fabric is washable, the linings may shrink.

Roman blinds are one simple option in a kitchen. There is very little fabric to trap dust and grime and they can be made in almost any fabric, and will create an impact on the design of a

DRAPING FABRIC

◄ If your kitchen has a private view you may decide not to use a curtain or blind and opt for a simple drape of fabric that frames the window instead. To achieve this effect, buy metal "spiral" holders that enable you to wind the fabric into attractive knots at each top corner.

room. They are also very simple to operate and are easily drawn up when not in use, making them less likely to get in the way of wall-mounted cabinets or sink and stove areas.

If you are the sort of person who tires of things easily, then a drape made of a simple square of fabric the size of your window recess will offer you the option of change. As you can see here, the same square has been attached to a window frame using ornate metal hooks, and it can be drawn up into a blind with two simple ties. The same drape can also be drawn to one side of the window to create a curtain using a tie.

Of course, fabric window treatments are not the only option. Wooden shutters and various forms of blind are also available – everything from the metal or wood Venetian blind to the simple rafia roller shade. Stained glass or shelves set into the window recess are alternative ways of creating privacy in a decorative manner without the use of traditional curtains and blinds.

CHECKS AND SQUARES

▼ This square of fabric is made of an unlined, large check cotton fabric, which has been framed with a border of the same fabric cut on the cross. It can easily be draw in to one side of the window and fastened with a tie.

Lighting

NIGHT LIGHTS
▲ Hardly anything can beat natural light, but at night discreet recessed halogen spots assisted by concealed under-cabinet lighting come into their own.

While most designers spend a great deal of time considering the correct combination of lighting for each room in the home, I suspect that the kitchen is the one room where most people would instinctively consider mixing different types of lighting. Common sense dictates that a kitchen should never be lit solely by a single central light as it will cast a shadow onto working areas and will not provide sufficient illumination. Many kitchens have a combination of central and under-unit concealed lighting, which is usually quite sufficient.

Fluorescent lighting has been used in domestic kitchens for many years. It is energy-efficient and gives out very little heat. However, the strips can sometimes emit a buzz and the light produced is very harsh and must be covered by a shade or shielded from the eye, since it can cause damage if you look directly into its light. Fluorescent bulbs are also expensive to dim as they require additional connections to achieve this.

Halogen lighting has become very popular in recent years. It takes its name from the fact that the bulb is filled with halogen gas, enabling it to reach very high temperatures, which creates a very white light. This is part of the attraction, as halogen lights produce true colors that do not distort.

Halogen spot- and recess lights are very small and unobtrusive, ideal for use with other forms of lighting. The bulbs are available in various strengths and widths of beam. This means you can use one bulb to create a wash of light while another can add a direct shaft of light using a narrow width of beam. However, take care when positioning halogen lights close to fabrics as they could be a fire hazard.

Tungsten has a shorter life expectancy than either fluorescent or halogen bulbs; it doesn't emit too much heat and is easily dimmed. However, tungsten bulbs produce a mellow, slightly yellow light, which is more true than fluorescent but it does sometimes affect the color of furnishings in the absence of natural light.

Install light switches at elbow height so they can easily be flicked on or off if your hands are full. Two-way switches are also essential if you have both an outside and inside door.

CONCEALED STRIPS
▲ The interesting shafts of light reflected in the metal backsplashes are produced by short lengths of concealed track lighting.

SNAKING LIGHTS
◀ This contemporary kitchen is enhanced by modern halogen light fixtures, which offer peaks of directional lighting.

Acknowledgments

The author and publishers would like to thank the following companies and their PR agencies for their kind assistance in the loan of photographs and props used in this book. We have taken care to ensure that we have acknowledged everyone and we apologize if, in error, we have omitted anyone.

For their kind loan of props:
Chloe Gardner, tile, page 16; Charles Harden, door knobs, page 20; Delaine Le Bas, blind, page 30; Jenny King, flower swag, page 39; Moira Neal, Lynda Howarth, painted glass, page 53; Heather Luke, blind, page 75.

For use of transparencies:
Alno Kitchens: page 11br, 33, 47b; Andrew Macintosh Furniture: pages 9b; 22b, 70, 71t; Atag: page 6t, 9t; Bisque radiators: page 25b; Blanco UK: 68t; Fired Earth: page 63b, 65t and b; Formica: page 67t; Hickman & Associates: page 11bl, Mark Wilkinson kitchens: pages 20–21; MFI: pages 38, 49t and b, 73; Nolte Kitchens: pages 25t, 61, 72; PJ Leiderer Industrie: page 67b; Smallbone of Devizes: pages 19, 41b, 57; Stanley Cookers: pages 45t; Wellmann Contessa: pages 13b, 22t; William Ball: page 8.

Picture Credits:
Abode: title page, pages 7, 10, 29, 35b, 37t, 51b, 64, 66, 72t, 74, 75t
C. Simon Sykes/The Interior Archive: pages 42, 44
Elizabeth Whiting Associates: pages 17, 35t, 52, 59;
Henry Wilson/The Interior Archive: pages 12, 23b, 43b, 62
J. Pilkington/The Interior Archive: pages 15, 43t
Ray Main/Mainstream Photography: cover, pages 5, 11tl and r, 76, 77b
Schulenburg/The Interior Archive: pages 13t, 24, 31, 50, 51t, 63t, 69, 77t
Simon Brown/The Interior Archive: pages 6b, 26, 68b
Simon Upton/The Interior Archive: page 55
Tim Beddow/ The Interior Archive: page 23t, 34

Index